READ WELL®

W9-CAW-701

# Sweet Otter Friends

# Teacher's Guide

### Read Well 1 · Unit 22

O o

O says /ooo/.
Continuous Sound
Voiced (Short)

Marilyn Sprick, Lisa Howard, Ann Fidanque, Shelley V. Jones

Copyright 2007 (Second Edition) Sopris West Educational Services. All rights reserved.

ISBN 13-digit: 978-1-59318-445-2     ISBN 10-digit: 1-59318-445-X     131941/4-13

11  12  13  14  15  RRDHRBVA  17  16  15  14  13

Cambium
LEARNING®
Group

Voyager
LEARNING

# Table of Contents
## Unit 22
## Sweet Otter Friends

### How to Teach the Lessons (*continued*)

### End of the Unit

| | | | | | |
|---|---|---|---|---|---|
| **I** /I/ Voiced (Word) **Unit A** | **Mm** /mmm/ **Monkey** Continuous Voiced **Unit B** | **Ss** /sss/ **Snake** Continuous Unvoiced **Unit 1** | **Ee** /eee/ **Emu** Continuous Voiced (Long) **Unit 2** | **ee** /eeee/ **Bee** Continuous Voiced (Long) **Unit 2** | **Mm** /mmm/ **Monkey** Continuous Voiced **Unit 3** |
| **Aa** /aaa/ **Ant** Continuous Voiced (Short) **Unit 4** | **Dd** /d/ **Dinosaur** Quick Voiced (not duh) **Unit 5** | **th** /ththth/ **the** Continuous Voiced **Unit 6** | **Nn** /nnn/ **Nest** Continuous Voiced **Unit 7** | **Tt** /t/ **Turkey** Quick Unvoiced (not tuh) **Unit 8** | **Ww** /www/ **Wind** Continuous Voiced (woo) **Unit 9** |
| **Ii** /iii/ **Insects** Continuous Voiced (Short) **Unit 10** | **Th** /Ththth/ **The** Continuous Voiced **Unit 10** | **Hh** /h/ **Hippo** Quick Unvoiced (not huh) **Unit 11** | **Cc** /c/ **Cat** Quick Unvoiced (not cuh) **Unit 12** | **Rr** /rrr/ **Rabbit** Continuous Voiced **Unit 13** | **ea** /eaeaea/ **Eagle** Continuous Voiced (Long) **Unit 13** |
| **Sh/sh** /shshsh/ **Sheep** Continuous Unvoiced **Unit 14** | **Kk, -ck** /k/ **Kangaroo** Quick Unvoiced (not kuh) **Unit 15** | **oo** /oooo/ **Moon** Continuous Voiced (Long) **Unit 16** | **ar** /ar/ **Shark** Voiced (R-Controlled) **Unit 17** | **Wh/wh** /wh/ **Whale** Quick Voiced **Unit 18** | **Ee** /ĕĕĕ/ **Engine or Ed** Continuous Voiced (Short) **Unit 19** |
| **-y** /-yyy/ **Fly** Continuous Voiced (Long) **Unit 20** | **Ll** /lll/ **Letter** Continuous Voiced **Unit 21** | **Oo** /ooo/ **Otter** Continuous Voiced (Short) **Unit 22** | **Bb** /b/ **Bat** Quick Voiced (not buh) **Unit 23** | **all** /all/ **Ball** Voiced **Unit 23** | **Gg** /g/ **Gorilla** Quick Voiced (not guh) **Unit 24** |
| **Ff** /fff/ **Frog** Continuous Unvoiced **Unit 25** | **Uu** /uuu/ **Umbrella** Continuous Voiced (Short) **Unit 26** | **er** /er/ **Sister** Voiced (R-Controlled) **Unit 27** | **oo** /oo/ **Book** Voiced (Short) **Unit 27** | **Yy** /y-/ **Yarn** Quick Voiced **Unit 28** | **Aa** /a/ **Ago** Voiced (Schwa) **Unit 28** |
| **Pp** /p/ **Pig** Quick Unvoiced (not puh) **Unit 29** | **ay** /ay/ **Hay** Voiced **Unit 29** | **Vv** /vvv/ **Volcano** Continuous Voiced **Unit 30** | **Qu/qu** /qu/ **Quake** Quick Unvoiced **Unit 31** | **Jj** /j/ **Jaguar** Quick Voiced (not juh) **Unit 32** | **Xx** /ksss/ **Fox** Continuous Unvoiced **Unit 33** |
| **or** /or/ **Horn** Voiced (R-Controlled) **Unit 33** | **Zz** /zzz/ **Zebra** Continuous Voiced **Unit 34** | **a_e** /a_e/ **Cake** Bossy E Voiced (Long) **Unit 34** | **-y** /-y/ **Baby** Voiced **Unit 35** | **i_e** /i_e/ **Kite** Bossy E Voiced (Long) **Unit 35** | **ou** /ou/ **Cloud** Voiced **Unit 36** |
| **ow** /ow/ **Cow** Voiced **Unit 36** | **Ch/ch** /ch/ **Chicken** Quick Unvoiced **Unit 37** | **ai** /ai/ **Rain** Voiced (Long) **Unit 37** | **igh** /igh/ **Flight** Voiced (Long) **Unit 38** | **o_e** /o_e/ **Bone** Bossy E Voiced (Long) **Unit 38** | **ir** /ir/ **Bird** Voiced (R-Controlled) **Unit 38** |

# Introduction
## Sweet Otter Friends

## Story Notes

Birthday celebrations are both exciting and a little anxiety producing for young children. Join Otto Otter as he relaxes and enjoys his first birthday party with a scavenger hunt. The children will have fun following the antics of Otto and his friends as they follow written clues to the big birthday treat.

## Recommended Read Aloud

For reading outside of small group instruction

### *Toot & Puddle* by Holly Hobbie

### Fiction

*Toot & Puddle* captures the imagination of young and old with cheerful postcards from one friend to another. As Toot travels, he sends news from around the world to his homebody friend, Puddle. At the story's end, the pigs reunite and celebrate their friendship and their differences. The children's enthusiasm for letter writing will grow as each treasured postcard is read.

### *Read Well* Connection

The *Read Well* stories in Units 21 and 22 are written around a theme of written communication. Just as the children look forward to each postcard in *Toot & Puddle*, Otto and his friends look forward to the written clues in their scavenger hunt.

**NOTE FROM THE AUTHORS**

**TARGETED PRACTICE MAKES PERFECT**

Confidence comes from high rates of success. With each succeeding unit, children are mastering the basics of reading. To maintain confidence, keep practice focused on passages composed of the sounds learned.

# New and Important Objectives
## A Research-Based Reading Program
### Just Right for Young Children

Oral Language
Phonemic Awareness
Phonics
Fluency
Vocabulary
Comprehension

### ◆◆ **Oral Language**

In Units 21–38, language patterns are provided for high-frequency words and for the low-frequency words that are likely to require clarification for many children. For English Language Learners and children with language delays, see page 10 for a list of the new high-frequency patterns.

### **Phonemic Awareness**

Isolating Beginning, Middle, Ending Sounds, Segmenting, Blending, Manipulating, Rhyming, Onset and Rime

O says /ooo/.
Otter on a log,
/O/, /o/, /ooo/.

Continuous Sound

## Phonics

### **Letter Sounds, Combinations, and Affixes**

☆*Oo*, ☆*cl-*, ☆*tw-*, ☆*-le*

Review • *Ss, Ee, ee, Mm, Aa, Dd, th, Nn, Tt, Ww, Ii, Th, Hh, Cc, Rr, ea, sh, Sh, Kk, -ck, oo, ar, wh, Wh, e (short), -y (as in "fly"), Ll*

### **Pattern Words**

☆*clam*, ☆*clams*, ☆*clean*, ☆*clock*, ☆*cost*, ☆*cot*, ☆*doodle*, ☆*dot*, ☆*hidden*, ☆*hot*, ☆*lend*, ☆*loss*, ☆*lost*, ☆*lot*, ☆*mom*, ☆*moss*, ☆*moth*, ☆*needle*, ☆*nodded*, ☆*not*, ☆*Not*, ☆*on*, ☆*rattle*, ☆*rock*, ☆*rocks*, ☆*Rod*, ☆*seal*, ☆*seals*, ☆*settle*, ☆*shell*, ☆*shoots*, ☆*slam*, ☆*sleek*, ☆*smooth*, ☆*Tess*, ☆*tot*, ☆*twist*

Review • *An, and, at, At, can, can't, card, cool, crack, dad, did, didn't, eat, Eat, eats, Eats, hard, hat, he, He, hear, hid, hit, hoot, I, I'm, in, ink, it, It, it's, It's, land, last, let, Let's, *little, man, mat, me, Me, meat, meet, Meet, met, Mom, my, neat, need, Need, needs, noon, read, Read, rest, room, Sam, sand, sea, Seal, Seals, see, See, she, She, shoot, shy, Sid, smack, Smack, smell, snack, Soon, started, still, swam, sweet, swell, swim, swims, swish, swoosh, Tee hee, tell, thanks, Thanks, that, That, That's, them, then, Then, thick, think, Think, this, This, three, too, treat, we, We, well, Well, wet, whack, Whack, wham, whoosh, will, with, With*

---

*Note: Occasionally a Tricky Word (e.g., "little") will be gradually moved from the Tricky Word category to the Pattern Word category as a pattern is established.

◆◆ = Oral language patterns　　☆ = New in this unit

## Phonics *(continued)*

### Tricky Words

☆*camel,* ☆*listen,* ☆*Listen,* ☆*mammal,* ☆*mammals,* ☆*otter,* ☆*Otter,* ☆*otters,* ☆*Otters,*
☆*Otto,* ☆*Otto's*

Review • *a, A, are, as, As, could, do, has, hasn't, his, I, into, is, Is, isn't, look, Look, one, said, should, the,
The, there, There, to, two, Two, wants, was, wasn't, what, What, where, Where, Who*

## Comprehension

### Comprehension Strategies

Building Knowledge, Priming Background Knowledge, Making Connections, Predicting,
Identifying, Describing, Defining, Applying, Explaining, Inferring, Affirming, Classifying,
Responding, Visualizing, Questioning, Summarizing

### Story Elements

Title, Who (Character), Want (Goal), What (Action)

### Story Vocabulary

☆Otter, ☆Celebration, ☆Clue

### Expository Text Elements

Fact, ☆Topic—Headings

### Genre

Nonfiction • Expository
Fiction • Narrative With Factual Content

### Lessons

Facts can help you identify and classify mammals. (First introduced in Unit 11)
Each animal has its own way of adapting to its environment. (First introduced in Unit 13)
☆Learn how to use clues. They will help you find things.

### Written Response

Sentence Completion, Sentence Writing, Sentence Comprehension—Multiple Choice,
Conventions—Periods, Capitals (Beginning of a Sentence), Quotation Marks

## Fluency

Accuracy, Expression, Phrasing, Rate

# Daily Lesson Planning

### PACING

Some students will begin the process of learning to read slowly but make rapid progress later. To be at grade level by the end of the year, most first graders need to complete Unit 30 by the end of the 27th week of school. Groups that are working at a slower pace may require more intensive *Read Well* instruction and practice. (See *Getting Started: A Guide to Implementation.*)

**A BASIC RULE**
**(Reminder)**
Make adjustments frequently, moving students as quickly as possible without sacrificing mastery.

### ASSESSMENT

Upon completion of this unit, assess each student and proceed to Unit 23 as appropriate.

### SAMPLE LESSON PLANS

The sample lesson plans illustrate how materials can be used for students with different learning needs. Each lesson plan is designed to provide daily decoding practice and story reading.

---

## 2-DAY PLAN • *Acceleration*

| **Day 1** | **Day 2** |
|---|---|
| • Decoding Practice 1 | • Decoding Practice 2 |
| • Stories 1 and 2 and Fact Summary | • Stories 3 and 5 |
| • Comprehension Work 1b* | • Comprehension Work 3* |
| • Comprehension Work 2a* | • Comprehension Work 5* |
| • Homework 1, Story 2* | • Homework 2, Story 4* |
| | • Homework 3, Story 6* |

In this 2-Day Plan, students skip Decoding Practice 3 and Stories 4 and 6. (Stories 4 and 6 are included in the homework schedule.) Do not assign Comprehension Work 6 unless students have read the story.)

*Important Note:* Introduce the Tricky Word "Listen" before Story 5.

---

## 3-DAY PLAN

| **Day 1** | **Day 2** | **Day 3** |
|---|---|---|
| • Decoding Practice 1 | • Decoding Practice 2 | • Decoding Practice 3 |
| • Stories 1 and 2 and Fact Summary | • Stories 3 and 4 | • Stories 5 and 6 |
| • Comprehension Work 1b* | • Comprehension Work 3* | • Comprehension Work 5* |
| • Comprehension Work 2a* | • Skill Work 4* | • Comprehension Work 6* |
| • Homework 1, Story 2* | • Homework 2, Story 4* | • Homework 3, Story 6* |
| | | • Homework 4, Storybook Decoding Review* |

To avoid excessive seatwork, 2-, 3-, and 4-Day Plans omit or adjust use of Skill Work. If appropriate, Skill Work 1a, 2b, and 4 can be used anytime during or after this unit as independent work or homework.

---

## 4-DAY PLAN

| **Day 1** | **Day 2** | **Day 3** | **Day 4** |
|---|---|---|---|
| • Decoding Practice 1 | • Decoding Practice 2 | • Decoding Practice 3 | • Decoding Practice 4 |
| • Stories 1 and 2 and Fact Summary | • Stories 3 and 4 | • Stories 5 and 6 | • Review Stories 2, 4, and 6 |
| • Comprehension Work 1b* | • Comprehension Work 3* | • Comprehension Work 5* | • Comprehension Work 6* |
| • Comprehension Work 2a* | • Skill Work 4* | • Homework 3, Story 6* | • Homework 4, Storybook Decoding Review* |
| • Homework 1, Story 2* | • Homework 2, Story 4* | | |

---

* From *Read Well* Comprehension and Skill Work (workbook), *Read Well* Homework (blackline masters), or Extra Practice in this book.

## 6-DAY PLAN • Pre-Intervention

| Day 1 | Day 2 | Day 3 |
|---|---|---|
| • Decoding Practice 1<br>• Story 1<br>• Skill Work 1a* (Optional)<br>• Comprehension Work 1b* | • Review Decoding Practice 1<br>• Story 2 and Fact Summary<br>• Comprehension Work 2a*<br>• Skill Work 2b* (Optional)<br>• Homework 1, Story 2* | • Decoding Practice 2<br>• Story 3<br>• Comprehension Work 3* |
| **Day 4** | **Day 5** | **Day 6** |
| • Review Decoding Practice 2<br>• Story 4<br>• Comprehension Work 4*<br>• Homework 2, Story 4* | • Decoding Practice 3<br>• Story 5<br>• Comprehension Work 5*<br>• Homework 4, Storybook Decoding Review* | • Decoding Practice 4<br>• Story 6<br>• Comprehension Work 6*<br>• Homework 3, Story 6* |

**PRE-INTERVENTION AND INTERVENTION**

See *Getting Started: A Guide to Implementation* for information on how to achieve mastery at a faster pace with students who require six or more days of instruction.

## 8-DAY PLAN • Intervention

| Day 1 | Day 2 | Day 3 | Day 4 |
|---|---|---|---|
| • Decoding Practice 1<br>• Story 1<br>• Skill Work 1a* (Optional)<br>• Comprehension Work 1b* | • Review Decoding Practice 1<br>• Story 2 and Fact Summary<br>• Comprehension Work 2a*<br>• Skill Work 2b* (Optional)<br>• Homework 1, Story 2* | • Decoding Practice 2<br>• Story 3<br>• Comprehension Work 3* | • Review Decoding Practice 2<br>• Story 4<br>• Comprehension Work 4*<br>• Homework 2, Story 4* |
| **Day 5** | **Day 6** | **Day 7** | **Day 8** |
| • Decoding Practice 3<br>• Story 5<br>• Comprehension Work 5*<br>• Homework 4, Storybook Decoding Review* | • Decoding Practice 4<br>• Story 6<br>• Comprehension Work 6*<br>• Homework 3, Story 6* | • Extra Practice 1*<br>• Extra Practice Activity 1* | • Extra Practice 2*<br>• Extra Practice 2 Fluency Passage* |

## 10-DAY PLAN • Intervention

| Day 1 | Day 2 | Day 3 | Day 4 | Day 5 |
|---|---|---|---|---|
| • Decoding Practice 1<br>• Story 1<br>• Skill Work 1a* (Optional)<br>• Comprehension Work 1b* | • Review Decoding Practice 1<br>• Story 2 and Fact Summary<br>• Comprehension Work 2a*<br>• Skill Work 2b* (Optional)<br>• Homework 1, Story 2* | • Decoding Practice 2<br>• Story 3<br>• Comprehension Work 3* | • Review Decoding Practice 2<br>• Story 4<br>• Comprehension Work 4*<br>• Homework 2, Story 4* | • Decoding Practice 3<br>• Story 5<br>• Comprehension Work 5*<br>• Homework 4, Storybook Decoding Review* |
| **Day 6** | **Day 7** | **Day 8** | **Day 9** | **Day 10** |
| • Decoding Practice 4<br>• Story 6<br>• Comprehension Work 6*<br>• Homework 3, Story 6* | • Extra Practice 1*<br>• Extra Practice Activity 1* | • Extra Practice 2*<br>• Extra Practice 2 Fluency Passage* | • Extra Practice 3*<br>• Extra Practice Activity 3* | • Extra Practice 4*<br>• Extra Practice Activity 4* |

# Materials and Materials Preparation

 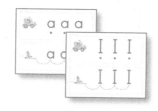   

## Core Lessons

### Teacher Materials

**READ WELL MATERIALS**

- Unit 22 Teacher's Guide
- Sound and Word Cards for Units 1–22
- Game markers (optional for use with cover-up activities)
- *Assessment Manual* or page 56

**SCHOOL SUPPLIES**

- Stopwatch or watch with a second hand

### Student Materials

**READ WELL MATERIALS**

- Decoding Book 2 for each student
- Unit 22 Storybook for each student
- Unit 22 Comprehension and Skill Work for each student (My Activity Book 2)
- Unit 22 Certificate of Achievement (blackline master page 57)
- Unit 22 Homework for each student (blackline masters)
  See *Getting Started* for suggested homework routines.

**SCHOOL SUPPLIES**

- Pencils, colors (optional—markers, crayons, or colored pencils)

Make one copy per student of each blackline master as appropriate for the group.

*Note:* For new or difficult Comprehension and Skill Work activities, make overhead transparencies from the blackline masters. Use the transparencies to demonstrate and guide practice.

## Extra Practice Lessons

**Note:** Use these lessons only if needed.

### Student Materials

**READ WELL MATERIALS**

- Unit 22 Extra Practice 1 and 2 for each student (blackline master pages 59 and 63)
- Unit 22 Extra Practice Activities 1, 2, 3, and 4 for each student (blackline master pages 60–61 double-sided; 64 single-sided; 66–67 single-sided; 68 single-sided)

**SCHOOL SUPPLIES**

- Pencils, colors (markers, crayons, or colored pencils), highlighters, scissors, glue
- White boards or paper

# Important Tips

## In this section, you will find:

★ **Reading for Information—Using Headings to Identify Subtopics**

With this unit, children begin learning to read for information, using headings to preview and review information learned.

★ **Jell-Well Reviews—Units 21–38**

When children enter school with little or no literacy background, or are among the few children for whom learning to read is very difficult, a periodic review of earlier units is sometimes necessary.

★ **Language and Vocabulary Practice— "Mammal" and High-Frequency Words**

An additional focus on vocabulary and language skills often benefits English Language Learners and students with language delays.

Preview the vocabulary word "mammal" before story reading. Recursive use of the word "mammal" provides students with an opportunity to increase their knowledge of the word, and an opportunity to continue practicing the skill of classifying.

A list of oral language patterns used with high-frequency words is also provided for additional emphasis and practice across settings.

# ★ Reading for Information
# Using Headings to Identify Subtopics

**PURPOSE**

With this unit, children continue learning to read for information. In previous units, children have had multiple opportunities to identify topics (what a nonfiction passage is about) and to identify facts.

Beginning with Unit 22, students will learn to use headings to preview and review what information will be learned. Instruction is explicit. You will demonstrate and then guide practice across multiple units as children begin learning basic strategies for working with nonfiction text structures.

**HEADINGS**

After students read the underlined heading "What are otters?" say something like:

The underlined words are called a heading. The words tell you what we will read about next. Read the underlined words again.

(What are otters?)

You are going to learn what otters are.

Demonstration ⟶ What will you learn? (What otters are)

**HEADINGS**

Before students read, have them find the two headings on this page. Say something like:

Find the first heading on this page. Read the underlined words.

(Where can we see sea otters?)

What will you learn?

Guided Practice ⟶ (Where we can see sea otters)

Find the next heading. It's in small print, so I'll read it. The heading says "How do otters stay warm?"

Repeated
Independent What else will we learn about on this page?
Practice ⟶ (How otters stay warm)

After students read the passage, they will summarize what they have learned and refer back to the headings to verify or affirm information learned.

# ★Jell-Well Reviews—Units 21–38

## PURPOSE

For children who begin learning to read with less literacy preparation and skill, a periodic review is sometimes critical to move forward.

## WHEN TO DO A JELL-WELL REVIEW

When a child or group of children receive a Weak Pass for two consecutive units, provide a Jell-Well Review. A Jell-Well Review for a group can often allow more rapid progress through later units.

## PROCEDURES

Determine when the individual child or the group last received Strong Passes. Go back to this unit and proceed forward again—as rapidly as possible. Develop daily Jell-Well lessons that include:

- **Sound and Word Card Practice**

  Practice known sounds with a special emphasis on vowels.

- **Accuracy and Fluency Building**

  Have students work daily on the words found in the Accuracy and Fluency columns in Decoding Practice 4. Use the Accuracy columns to build discrimination (lick, lack, look, luck) and the Fluency columns to build speed of recognition (lick, sick, Nick, Rick).

- **Word Practice**

  Have students work in the Decoding Practice. Incorporate dictation, word building, and blending games in your practice. (See *Getting Started: A Guide to Implementation* and examples from the Teacher's Guides.)

- **Daily Solo Story Reading With Repeated Readings**

  Provide daily repeated readings of Solo Stories from the review unit. Homework and Extra Practice provide excellent resources. (Some teachers copy the Homework to create Solo Story notebooks.)

## LESSON PLANNER

A Jell-Well Lesson Planner and more detailed information can be found in *Getting Started: A Guide to Implementation* and in the *Assessment Manual*.

# Language and Vocabulary Practice "Mammal" and High-Frequency Words

**◆◆ FOR ENGLISH LANGUAGE LEARNERS AND CHILDREN WITH LANGUAGE DELAYS**

## PURPOSE

Additional language lessons around selected vocabulary words prior to story reading build comprehension. Continued use of the word after story reading will also increase word knowledge and understanding across settings. The following lessons may be used to augment a structured oral language program.

## PREVIEW "MAMMAL" BEFORE READING UNIT 22

In Unit 22, students expand their knowledge of mammals by learning about sea otters and seals.

- Collect pictures of sea mammals with their babies.
- Using the pictures, say something like:
  Let's see if we can remember the four facts we learned earlier in the year about *mammals*. Mammals have a . . . **Point to the mammal's backbone** . . . (backbone).
  Mammals breathe . . . **Point to the mammal's nose** . . . (air).
  Mammals have hair or . . . **Point to the mammal's fur** . . . (fur).
  Mammals take care of their . . . **Point to the mammal's baby** . . . (babies).
  Animals that have a backbone and hair or fur, breathe air, and take care of their babies are called . . . (*mammals*).
  Does a [seal] have a backbone?  (Yes)
  Does a [seal] breathe air?  (Yes)
  Does a [seal] have fur?  (Yes)
  Does a [seal] take care of its babies?  (Yes)
  So, what is a seal?  (A mammal)

## REVIEW "MAMMAL" AFTER READING UNIT 22

Review the word and classification of mammals using pictures of various animals.

## ORAL LANGUAGE PATTERNS USED WITH HIGH-FREQUENCY WORDS

*Read Well* Decoding Practice includes simple sentences for all new high-frequency words. The language patterns are repeated below for additional practice.

| ORAL LANGUAGE PATTERNS |
|---|
| ☆High-Frequency Words Introduced in This Unit |
| ☆After you wash your hands, they are . . . *clean.* |
| ☆This is *not* a [pencil]. Is this a [pencil]?  (No, this is *not* a [pencil].) |
| ☆The [book] is *on* the [table]. Where is the [book]?  (*On* the [table]) |

# How to Teach the Lessons

Teach from this section. Each instructional component is outlined in an easy-to-teach format. Special tips are provided to help you nurture student progress.

## Decoding Practice 1

- Unit Introduction
- Story 1, Duet
- Skill Work Activity 1a
- Comprehension Work Activity 1b

- Story 2, Solo
- Fact Summary
- Comprehension Work Activity 2a
- Skill Work Activity 2b

## Decoding Practice 2

- Story 3, Duet
- Comprehension Work Activity 3

- Story 4, Solo
- Skill Work Activity 4

## Decoding Practice 3

- Story 5, Duet
- Comprehension Work Activity 5

- Story 6, Solo
- Comprehension Work Activity 6

## Decoding Practice 4

Review Solo Stories

---

**BUILDING INDEPENDENCE**
**Next Steps • Principles of Instruction**

For Units 21–38, follow the scaffolded principles of instruction below.

Provide demonstration and/or guided practice only with:
- New sounds
- Pattern words with new sounds
- New Tricky Words
- New multisyllabic words

Provide independent practice (practice without your assistance or voice) on:
- New and review pattern words with known sounds
- Review Tricky Words
- Review multisyllabic words

If students make errors, provide appropriate corrections.
- Have students identify any difficult sound and then sound out the word. Provide discrimination practice.
- Reintroduce difficult Tricky Words based on the initial introduction procedures.

If students require your assistance on words with known sounds, evaluate placement and consider a Jell-Well Review.

**① SOUND REVIEW**

Use selected Sound Cards from Units 1–21.

**② NEW SOUND INTRODUCTION**

- Before reading the poem, write oo on the board and ask students to tell you the sound.
- Then, erase the second o and say something like:
  Today we are going to learn what *one* letter o often says. Listen to the poem.
- Have students echo the poem for "O as in Otter."
- When you are finished, point to the single letter o on the board and say something like:
  What sound does *one* letter o often make? (/ŏŏŏ/)

**③ NEW SOUND PRACTICE**

◆◆ **④ FOCUS ON VOCABULARY**

**Review vocabulary word: "mammal"**

Have students review the word "mammal" and use it in a sentence. Say something like:
Let's see if we can remember the four facts we've learned about *mammals*.
Mammals have a . . . **Point to your backbone** . . . (backbone). Mammals breathe . . . (air).
Mammals have hair or . . . (fur). Mammals take care of their . . . (babies).
Look at the picture. An otter is a . . . *(mammal)*.

◆◆ **⑤ SOUNDING OUT SMOOTHLY**

- For each word, have students say the underlined part, sound out the word, and then read the word. Use the words in sentences as needed.
- Provide repeated practice. Mix group and individual turns, independent of your voice.

**⑥ ACCURACY AND FLUENCY BUILDING**

◆◆ ☆ **New blend: /cl-/**

- For each column, have students say any underlined part, then read each word.
- Have students read the whole column.
- Repeat practice on each column, building accuracy first and then fluency.

*Note:* If students have difficulty with /cl-/ in the Flower Column, write "am" on the chalkboard and have students read "am." Add an l and have students read "lam." Then add a c and have students read "clam." Repeat with "ock-lock-clock," and "ean-lean-clean."

**⑦ TRICKY WORDS**

☆ **New Tricky Word: "otters"**

The word "otters" will be a pattern word once students learn er (Unit 27). For now, however, say something like: Your new Tricky Word is "otters." Listen to me sound out "otters." /ŏŏŏterzzz/
Later you will learn that er says /er/. Now read the word. (otters)

Have students read the row. Repeat, mixing group and individual turns, independent of your voice.

**⑧ DAILY STORY READING**

Proceed to the Unit 22 Storybook. See Daily Lesson Planning for pacing suggestions.

**⑨ COMPREHENSION AND SKILL WORK ACTIVITY I AND/OR ACTIVITY 2**

See pages 20–21 and/or 26–27.

UNIT **22** DECODING PRACTICE 1
(For use with Stories 1 and 2)

1. SOUND REVIEW  Use Sound Cards for Units 1–21.

2. NEW SOUND INTRODUCTION  Have the students echo (repeat) the phrases. Do not have students read the poem.

O as in Otter
Capital letter O, small letter o,
O says ooo.
Otter on a log,
O, o, ooo.

3. NEW SOUND PRACTICE  Have students read, trace, and say /ooo/.

4. FOCUS ON VOCABULARY  See the Teacher's Guide for detailed instructions.

O  o

★mammal

**SHORT VOWEL E**
Diacritical marks are gradually phased out of the Decoding Practice. If your students have difficulty, you might give them transparencies and have them draw the "smiles" over the short vowel e.

5. SOUNDING OUT SMOOTHLY  For each word, have students say the underlined part, sound out the word in one smooth breath, and then read the word.

▲

on     not     mom     rock

★6. ACCURACY/FLUENCY BUILDING  For each column, have students say any underlined part, then read each word. Next, have students read the column.

| ✈ | ● | ✿ | ■ |
|---|---|---|---|
| smell | will | ★clam | crack |
| smack | well | clock | whack |
| smooth | shell | clean | snack |

**◆◆ SENTENCE SUGGESTIONS**

▲ on – The [book] is *on* the [table]. Where is the [book]?

▲ not – This is *not* a [pencil]. Is this a [pencil]?

✿ clean – After you wash your hands, they are . . . (*clean*).

★7. TRICKY WORDS  Introduce "otters" using the Tricky Word procedure. Next, have students silently figure out each word and then read it aloud.

☆

★otters     Look     one     should

8. DAILY STORY READING

49

Sentence Suggestions: If a sentence is included, use it *after* decoding the individual word. The sentences may be used to build oral language patterns and vocabulary. Use of sentences also emphasizes that words have meaning.

### ❶ INTRODUCING THE UNIT AND THE TITLE PAGE

**Identifying—Title**

Tell students this unit is called "Sweet Otter Friends."

**Priming Background Knowledge**

Ask students if they've ever seen an otter. Ask students what they already know about otters.

Explain that this unit includes a factual passage about otters and a made-up story about a little otter's birthday party.

### ❷ INTRODUCING VOCABULARY

**Vocabulary—Otter, Celebration, Clue**

*Otter*

Put your finger under the first picture.

An *otter* is a mammal that lives mostly in the water.

**Making Connections, Applying**

Since an otter is a mammal, you already know some facts about it.

What do you know about an otter?

*Celebration*

Put your finger under the next picture.

A *celebration* is often a party. A birthday party is a birthday celebration.

*Clue*

A *clue* is something that helps us find something.

In this story, the little otters will follow clues that they find in notes.

# Sweet Otter Friends

*Illustrated by Ashley Mims*

## Otters in the Sea
*By Marilyn Sprick*

## Otto's First Birthday Celebration
*By Jessica Sprick and Marilyn Sprick*

**UNIT 22 STORIES**

### Vocabulary Words

**otter**
An otter is a mammal that lives mostly in the water.

**celebration**
A celebration is often a party. A birthday party is a birthday celebration.

**clue**
A clue is something that helps us find something.

26          27

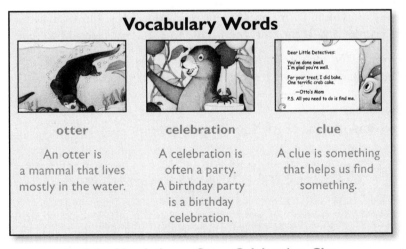

### Vocabulary Words

**otter**
An otter is a mammal that lives mostly in the water.

**celebration**
A celebration is often a party. A birthday party is a birthday celebration.

**clue**
A clue is something that helps us find something.

Dear Little Detectives:
You've done swell.
I'm glad you're well.

For your treat, I did bake,
One terrific crab cake.

—Otto's Mom
P.S. All you need to do is find me.

**Defining Vocabulary—Otter, Celebration, Clue**

### DUET STORY READING INSTRUCTIONS

Students read from their own storybooks.

The teacher reads the small text and students read the large text.

### PACING

- 2- to 4-Day Plans: Have students do the first reading of Duet Story 1.

  Then proceed to repeated readings of Solo Story 2.
- 6- to 10-Day Plans: Have students do the first *and* second readings as needed.

### COMPREHENSION BUILDING:
### DISCUSSION QUESTIONS AND TEACHER THINK ALOUDS

- Ask questions and discuss text on the first reading when indicated in the storybook in light gray text.
- Encourage students to answer questions with complete sentences when appropriate. Following a response, acknowledge the accuracy of the response and then say something like:

  Yes, a sea otter's habitat is the sea. Start your answer with "A sea otter's . . ."
  (A sea otter's habitat is the sea.)

- If students have difficulty with a comprehension question, think aloud with them or reread the portion of the story that answers the question. Then, ask the question again.

### PROCEDURES

**1. Introducing the Story**

Before reading the story, say something like:

This story is called "Otters in the Sea."

The chapter is called "Sea Otter Facts."

What will you learn in this chapter? (Facts about otters)

A fact is something that is real.

★ **2. First Reading**

Mix group and individual turns on student-read sentences. On individual turns, gently correct any error, and then have the student reread the text.

*Note:* In this unit, students are introduced to headings in a nonfiction passage. Watch the zebra notes for instructional procedures.

**3. Repeated Readings**

Repeat the reading only as needed for comprehension.

STORY 1, DUET

## Otters in the Sea

### CHAPTER 1
### Sea Otter Facts

Look at the sea otters.  See them swim in the sea.

**FINGER TRACKING**
**(Reminder)**
Continue having children track the large text with their fingers.

## What are otters?

**Otters are mammals.** Otters have backbones. They breathe air. They take care of their babies, and they have fur or hair.

Tell me five facts about otters. ❶

28

**HEADINGS**

After students read the underlined heading "What are otters?" say something like:

The underlined words are called a heading. The words tell you what we will read about next. Read the underlined words again. (What are otters?)

You are going to find out what otters are. What will you learn?  (What otters are)

❶ **Identifying—Facts** (Otters are mammals. They have backbones, breathe air, take care of their babies, and have fur.)

## HEADINGS

Before students read, have them find the two headings on this page. Say something like:

Find the first heading on this page. Read the underlined words. (Where can we see sea otters?)

What will you learn? (Where we can see sea otters)

Find the next heading. It's in small print, so I'll read it. The heading says "How do otters stay warm?" What else will we learn about on this page? (How otters stay warm)

# Where can we see sea otters?

## Not in the sand.  Not on the land.

## Otters swim, eat, and rest in the sea.

## Otters are sea mammals. A sea otter's habitat is the sea.

What is a sea otter's habitat?[1]

**How do otters stay warm?**

The sea is very cold, so an otter's fur is made up of millions of hairs.

## It is thick and smooth.

Look at the picture.  Tell me about an otter's fur.[2]

29

❶ **Explaining, Using Vocabulary—Habitat** (The sea otter's habitat is the sea.)

❷ **Describing** (It is thick and smooth.)

# What do otters eat?

Otters eat clams. They also eat fish, crab, and sea urchins. They dive deep into the ocean looking for food. Then they bring their food to the surface and eat it while lying on their backs. Have you ever tried to eat lying on your back? [1] What happens? [2]

### How do otters stay clean?

Otters roll in the water to play, but they also roll for another reason.

Otters are clean. As otters swim in the sea, the water washes off food and keeps the otters clean.

### How do otters learn to swim?

A little otter needs its mom. It can't swim well. It eats and swims with its mom. The otter mother cuddles, grooms, and teaches her baby until it is about six months old. Otter mothers take very good care of their babies.

What do otter mothers do? [3]

30

❶ **Making Connections**

❷ **Inferring, Explaining**

❸ **Identifying—What** (They cuddle, groom, and teach their babies.)

### SOUND PAGE

Use work pages from the workbook.

UNIT 22 SKILL WORK ACTIVITY 1a
SOUND PAGE: For use after Story 1
Name _____ ▲

O o

77

### PROCEDURES

For each step, demonstrate and guide practice as needed.

**1. Handwriting—Basic Instructions**
- Have students identify the capital letter O as in "Otter."
- Have students trace and write the capital letter O—leaving a finger space between each letter. Repeat with the small letter o on the last two rows.
- In each row, have students circle their best letter.

**2. Coloring—Basic Instructions**
- Have students color the picture of the otter, using at least three colors.

*Note:* Neat work helps students take pride in their efforts. Periodically, demonstrate how to produce "neat" work. Show students how to color in one direction and how to color the background. With individuals, comment on best efforts and improvements.

★ **FACT SHEET**

Use work pages from the workbook.

**CHECKOUT OPPORTUNITY**

Listen to your students read individually while others work.

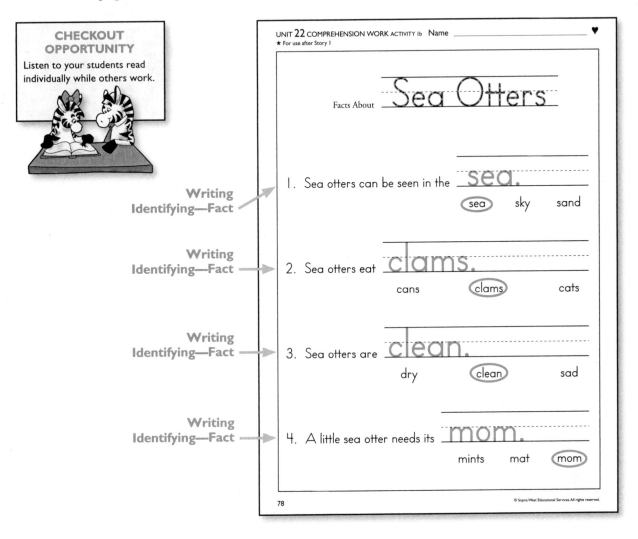

UNIT **22** COMPREHENSION WORK ACTIVITY 1b   Name _____
★ For use after Story 1

Facts About **Sea Otters**

Writing
Identifying—Fact

1. Sea otters can be seen in the **sea.**

(sea)   sky   sand

Writing
Identifying—Fact

2. Sea otters eat **clams.**

cans   (clams)   cats

Writing
Identifying—Fact

3. Sea otters are **clean.**

dry   (clean)   sad

Writing
Identifying—Fact

4. A little sea otter needs its **mom.**

mints   mat   (mom)

78

## PROCEDURES

For each step, demonstrate and guide practice as needed.

- (Demonstrate) Have students orally respond to items while you demonstrate how to complete the page.
- (Guide) Have students orally respond to the items, but do not demonstrate how to complete the page.
- (Independent With Support) Have students silently read over the items and ask any questions they may have.

**Multiple Choice, Sentence Completion—Basic Instructions**

- Remind students that a fact is something that is real. Tell them they are going to be writing facts about sea otters.
- Have students select and circle the word that correctly completes the sentence. Periodically, think aloud with students. Discuss the multiple choice options. As appropriate, ask questions like: "Does the first answer make sense?" "Is that what the book said?" "Is the answer completely correct?"
- Have them write answers in the blanks and place a period at the end.

*Note:* You may wish to remind students that they can look in their storybooks if they are unsure about the correct answer.

## SOLO STORY READING INSTRUCTIONS

Students read from their own storybooks.

## COMPREHENSION BUILDING:
## DISCUSSION QUESTIONS AND TEACHER THINK ALOUDS

- Ask questions and discuss text on the first reading when indicated in the storybook in light gray text.
- Encourage students to answer questions with complete sentences.
- If students have difficulty with a comprehension question, think aloud with them or reread the portion of the story that answers the question. Then, ask the question again.

## PROCEDURES

### 1. Review headings in Chapter 1.

Have students turn to Chapter 1. Quickly review a few of the underlined headings and what students learned.

### 2. First Reading

Mix group and individual turns on student-read sentences. On individual turns, gently correct any error, and then have the student reread the text.

After students complete the first reading and before the second reading, have students practice a paragraph. First demonstrate expressive reading for students, then give individual turns. Acknowledge student efforts.

### 3. Second Reading

- Mix group and individual turns, independent of your voice.
  Have students work toward an accuracy goal of 0–2 errors.
  Quietly keep track of errors made by all students in each group.
- After reading the story, practice any difficult words.
- If the group has not reached the accuracy goal, have the group reread the story, mixing group and individual turns.

### 4. Repeated Readings

#### a. Timed Readings

- Once the accuracy goal has been achieved, have individual students read the page while the other children track the text with their fingers and whisper read.
  Time individuals for 30 seconds and encourage each student to work for his or her personal best.
- Count the number of words read correctly in 30 seconds (words read minus errors).
  Multiply by two to determine words read correctly per minute. Record student scores.

*Note:* If a student is unable to read with close to 100% accuracy, the personal goal should be accuracy. If the student is unable to read with accuracy, evaluate group placement and consider a Jell-Well Review.

#### b. Partner Reading

During students' daily independent work, have them do Partner Reading.

#### c. Homework 1

Have students read the story at home. (A reprint of this story is available on a blackline master in *Read Well* Homework.)

## CHAPTER 2
# An Otter Eats

**HEADINGS**

After students read the chapter title, say something like:

Read the heading.
(What will the otter do with the clam?)
What will you learn about?
(What the otter will do with the clam)

## What will the otter do with the clam?

That sweet otter wants to eat that clam. He will hit the clam with a rock. He will hit it hard. With a smack and a whack, that shell will crack.

What does the otter want to eat?**1** How will he crack the clam shell?**2**

31

❶ **Identifying—What** (The otter wants to eat a clam.)

❷ **Explaining** (He will hit it with a rock.)

STORY 2, SOLO

Smack!  Whack!  That shell did crack.  At last the otter has his snack. He will eat his snack at sea.  Then he will swim in the sea.  He will swish and swoosh in the sea.

Where does the otter eat?[1] Then what does he do?[2]

32

❶ Identifying—**Where** (The otter eats at sea.)

❷ Identifying—**Action** (The otter swims in the sea.)

**QUESTIONING**
After students read the page, explore further questions. Say something like:

I think otters are very interesting. They like swimming in the sea. I'd like to learn where they sleep. I wonder if they sleep on land or in the sea.

What else would you like to learn about otters?

## COMPREHENSION BUILDING: FACT SUMMARY

Read the text. Then, have students orally answer each question.
For each question, have students turn back to the matching header
in Chapters 1 and 2. Reread the text to affirm student responses.

### Otters in the Sea

We learned many facts about sea otters. A fact tells something that
is real. Look at the pictures and answer the questions with facts you learned.[1]

1. **What are otters?**[2] Let's check your answer on p. 28.

2. **Where can we see sea otters?**[3] Let's check your answer on p. 29.

3. **How do otters stay warm?**[4] Let's check your answer on p. 29.

4. **What do otters eat?**[5] Let's check your answer on p. 30.

5. **What will the otter do with the clam?**[6] Let's check your answer on p. 31.

6. **What else would you like to learn about otters?**[7]

33

### QUESTION 1
### Affirming

After answering "What
are otters?" have students
turn to page 28 in their
storybooks. Say something
like:

Look at the heading under
the picture. What does it
say? (What are otters?)
That's where we can check
our answer. We said otters
were mammals. What
does it say? (Otters are
mammals.) Were we right?

Repeat the process with
the other questions as time
allows.

❶ **Building Knowledge**

❷ **Classifying** (Otters are mammals.)

❸ **Identifying—Where, Using Vocabulary—Habitat** (We can see otters in the sea.
Sea otters live in the sea. Their habitat is the sea.)

❹ **Explaining** (Otters have thick fur. Their fur is made up of millions of hairs.)

❺ **Identifying—What** (Otters eat clams, fish, crab, and sea urchins.)

❻ **Explaining** (The otter will hit the clam with a rock. The otter will break the shell with
a rock. Then he will eat the clam.)

❼ **Questioning**

### STORY COMPREHENSION

Use work pages from the workbook.

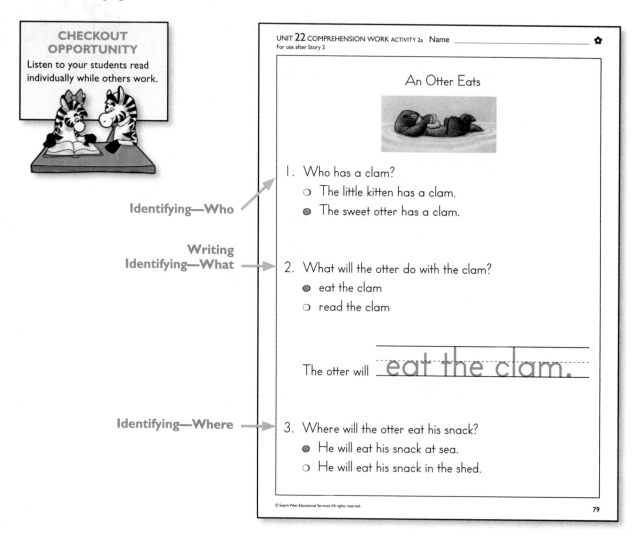

CHECKOUT OPPORTUNITY

Listen to your students read individually while others work.

Identifying—Who

Writing
Identifying—What

Identifying—Where

---

UNIT 22 COMPREHENSION WORK ACTIVITY 2a  Name _____
For use after Story 2

An Otter Eats

1. Who has a clam?
   ○ The little kitten has a clam.
   ● The sweet otter has a clam.

2. What will the otter do with the clam?
   ● eat the clam
   ○ read the clam

The otter will _eat the clam._

3. Where will the otter eat his snack?
   ● He will eat his snack at sea.
   ○ He will eat his snack in the shed.

79

---

### PROCEDURES

For each step, demonstrate and guide practice as needed.

**Multiple Choice, Sentence Completion—Basic Instructions**

- Have students fill in the bubble for the correct answer.
- Have them write an answer in the blank and place a period at the end.

*Note:* You may wish to remind students that they can look in their storybooks if they are unsure about the correct answer.

### ALPHABET DETECTIVE

Use work pages from the workbook.

**CHECKOUT OPPORTUNITY**

Listen to your students read individually while others work.

### PROCEDURES

For each step, demonstrate and guide practice as needed.

**1. Letter Find—Basic Instructions**

- Have students look at the first box at the top of the page and follow the directions. Ask:

  What letters will you look for? (The capital letter O and the small letter o)

  What will you do when you find a capital letter O or a small letter o? (Draw a triangle around it.)

- Have students look at the second box at the top of the page. Ask:

  What other letter will you look for? (The small letter l)

  What will you do when you find a small letter l? (Circle it.)

UNIT 22 SKILL WORK ACTIVITY 2b
ALPHABET DETECTIVE: For use after Story 2     Name _____

O as in Otter

Capital letter O, small letter o,

O says ooo.

Otter on a log,

O, o, ooo.

80                                    © Sopris West Educational Services. All rights reserved.

**2. Self-Monitoring—Basic Instructions**

Have students systematically check each line after finishing the task.

*Alternative:* At the beginning of the exercise, tell students the number of o's they will draw a triangle around and the number of l's they will circle. Have students write the numbers on the top of their papers. When students complete the activity, have them count the number of triangles and circles they have drawn. If the numbers are incorrect, they can recheck each line.

**3. Coloring—Optional**

Have students carefully color the picture, using at least three colors.

*Note:* If students have difficulty with the multi-step directions, have them do just the first step.

**1 SOUND REVIEW**

Use selected Sound Cards for Units 1–22 or the Sound Review on Decoding Practice 4.

**2 NEW SOUND PRACTICE**

◆◆ **3 FOCUS ON VOCABULARY**

⭐ **New vocabulary word: "celebration"**

Introduce the word "celebration" and give examples of its meaning. Say something like:

Your new vocabulary word is "celebration." Tell me your new word. (Celebration)

A *celebration* is often a party. A birthday party is a birthday . . . celebration.

A party to congratulate someone is called a celebration.

After the baseball team won the game, they had a . . . celebration.

**4 SOUNDING OUT SMOOTHLY**

- For each word, have students say any underlined part, sound out the word, and then read the word. Use the words in sentences as needed.
- Provide repeated practice. Mix group and individual turns, independent of your voice.

*Note:* For the word "mammal," tell students that they can sound out this big word that is made up of two parts. Have students sound out "mam," then "mal." Remind students that a letter with a slash through it doesn't say anything. Next, have students look at the equals sign. Say something like:

When you put the two little parts together, what big word does it make? (mammal)

Repeat with "camel."

**5 ACCURACY AND FLUENCY BUILDING**

⭐ **New consonant blend: /tw-/**

- For each column, have students say any underlined part, then read each word.
- Have students read the whole column.
- Repeat practice on each column, building accuracy first and then fluency.

*Note:* If students have difficulty with /tw-/ in the Triangle Column, write "ist" on the chalkboard and have students read "ist." Add a <u>w</u> and have students read "wist." Then add a <u>t</u> and have students read "twist."

**6 TRICKY WORDS**

⭐ **New Tricky Word: "Otto"**

- Have students look at their new Tricky Word, "Otto." Say something like:

Your new Tricky Word is "Otto." Otto is the name of an otter in your story.

We spell "Otto" <u>O</u>-t-t-<u>o</u>. Spell "Otto" with me. <u>O</u>-t-t-<u>o</u>

Spell "Otto" three times by yourselves. (<u>O</u>-t-t-<u>o</u>, <u>O</u>-t-t-<u>o</u>, <u>O</u>-t-t-<u>o</u>)

Touch the word "Otto" and read it. (Otto) The otter in our story is named . . . Otto.

- Have students read the row. Repeat, mixing group and individual turns.

**7 DAILY STORY READING**

Proceed to the Unit 22 Storybook. See Daily Lesson Planning for pacing suggestions.

**8 COMPREHENSION AND SKILL WORK ACTIVITY 3 AND/OR ACTIVITY 4**

See pages 35 and/or 39.

---

◆◆ For ELLs and children with language delays, provide repeated and extended practice with the language patterns. See page 10 for tips.

UNIT 22 DECODING PRACTICE 2
(For use with Stories 3 and 4)

1. SOUND REVIEW  Use Sound Cards for Units 1–22 or Sound Review on Decoding Practice 4.

2. NEW SOUND PRACTICE  Have students read, trace, and say /ooo/.

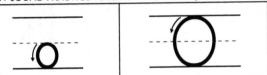

★3. FOCUS ON VOCABULARY  Introduce "celebration." See the Teacher's Guide for detailed instructions.

**TRICKY WORD CARDS**
**(Reminder)**

After the Sound Review, practice difficult Tricky Words with the Tricky Word Cards.

4. SOUNDING OUT SMOOTHLY  For each word, have students say any underlined part, sound out the word in one smooth breath, and then read the word.

● S<u>i</u>d    <u>s</u>eal    c<u>oo</u>l    <u>n</u>odded

■ mam·møl = mammal | cam·el = camel

**BUILDING INDEPENDENCE**
**(Reminder)**

Provide demonstration and guided practice only as needed. Students need opportunities to figure out new pattern words without your assistance.

★5. ACCURACY/FLUENCY BUILDING  For each column, have students say any underlined part, then read each word. Next, have students read the column.

▲ ★tw<u>i</u>st    ✈ m<u>o</u>m    ❀ wet
treat    n<u>o</u>t    let
sl<u>ee</u>k    R<u>o</u>d    lend
cl<u>am</u>s    land

◆◆ **SENTENCE SUGGESTIONS**

● nodded – Look at me. **Nod your head.** I *nodded* my head.

▲ twist – Everyone, stand up and show me how to . . . (*twist*).

▲ sleek – Something that is smooth and shiny is . . . (*sleek*).

✈ not – This is *not* a [pencil]. Is this a [pencil]?

★6. TRICKY WORDS  Introduce "Otto" using the Tricky Word procedure. Next, have students silently figure out each word and then read it aloud.

♥ ★Otto    otters    Who    there

7. DAILY STORY READING

50

Sentence Suggestions: Use the appropriate suggested sentence *after* decoding each individual word.

### DUET STORY READING INSTRUCTIONS

Students read from their own storybooks.
The teacher reads the small text and students read the large text.

### PACING

- 2- to 4-Day Plans: Have students do the first reading
  of Duet Story 3.
  Then, proceed to repeated readings of Solo Story 4.
- 6- to 10-Day Plans: Have students do the first *and*
  second readings as needed.

### COMPREHENSION BUILDING:
### DISCUSSION QUESTIONS AND TEACHER THINK ALOUDS

- Ask questions and discuss text on the first reading when indicated in
  the storybook in light gray text.
- Encourage students to answer questions with complete sentences.
- If students have difficulty with a comprehension question, think aloud
  with them or reread the portion of the story that answers the question.
  Then, ask the question again.

### PROCEDURES

**1. First Reading**

Mix group and individual turns on student-read sentences. On individual
turns, gently correct any error, and then have the student reread the text.

**2. Second Reading**

Repeat the reading only as needed for comprehension.

STORY 3, DUET

### Otto's First Birthday Celebration

What is a celebration?**1** What is Otto celebrating?**2**

## CHAPTER 1

### A Scavenger Hunt

What a great day! It was Otto's birthday, and his friends had gathered for a party. This was Otto's first party. Otto was a little nervous, but things had gone well. The little otters played Pin the Fin on the Fish and Go Fish.

At last, Otto's mom said, "I have a surprise for you. We have one more game to play. It's a scavenger hunt. You get to be detectives."

## The little otters said, "That's cool! That's neat! What do we do?"

Otto's mom said, "There are clues to follow. Follow the clues. At the end of the scavenger hunt, you will find a treat that can't be beat."

## Otto said, "A treat! Is it clams?"

## "Not clams," said Otto's mom.

What will the otters find at the end of the scavenger hunt?**3** That's their goal—to find the treat.**4**

34

**FOCUS ON VOCABULARY**
**Making Connections**
After completing the page, say something like: The otters are going to be detectives in this game. A detective finds things. What are the otters going to find? (They are going to find a treat.)

They will follow clues. What is a clue? (A clue is something that helps us find something.)

That sounds like a fun game. Have you ever played a game with clues?

❶ **Defining Vocabulary—Celebration** (A celebration is a party to congratulate someone.)

❷ **Identifying—What** (His first birthday)

❸ **Identifying—Goal** (The otters will find a treat.)

❹ **Teacher Think Aloud**

Otto's mom said, "Read this card."

The card said:

This is your first clue. Go find a mammal.

It isn't a camel!

We see this mammal

on the land *and* in the sea.
*This big creature has one strange feature—
its very large nose!*

Who can it be?
Listen again.
What do the otters need
to look for?❶ That's the
first clue.❷

35

❶ **Identifying—What** (A mammal that lives on the land and in the sea.)

❷ **Teacher Think Aloud, Using Vocabulary—Clue**

STORY 3, DUET

"This is fun," said Tess. "The clue is like a puzzle piece. An elephant has a very large nose, but an elephant doesn't live in the sea."

# Rod nodded. Then he said, "We need to think. This is hard!"

Otto said, "A whale is a mammal. It lives in the sea, but it doesn't live on the land. And, it doesn't have a large nose."

How does Otto know they aren't looking for a whale?[1]

36

❶ **Explaining** (It doesn't live on the land; it doesn't have a large nose.)

Then Tess said, "I think it's a seal!"

"It's not a seal," said Rod. "A seal doesn't have a big nose."

Why does Rod think it isn't a seal?[1]

Then Otto said, "I think it is a seal.

We need to see Sid Seal. Follow me."

For some reason, Otto thinks they are looking for a seal.[2] What do you think Otto knows about Sid Seal?[3]

37

### VISUALIZING

After reading the page, say something like: Close your eyes. Imagine the seals you've seen. Does the seal you are thinking of have a big nose? Otto thinks the clue is about Sid Seal. Do you think he is on the right track?

❶ **Explaining** (Most seals don't have big noses.)

❷ **Teacher Think Aloud**

❸ **Predicting, Inferring**

### STORY COMPREHENSION

Use work pages from the workbook.

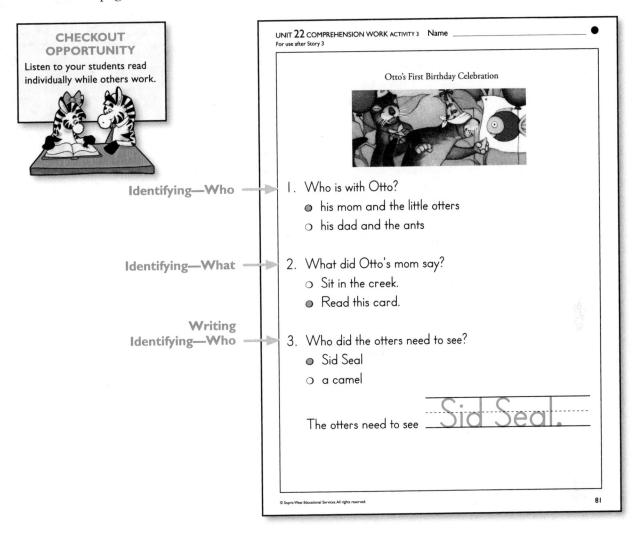

**CHECKOUT OPPORTUNITY**

Listen to your students read individually while others work.

Identifying—Who

Identifying—What

Writing
Identifying—Who

UNIT 22 COMPREHENSION WORK ACTIVITY 3  Name _____
For use after Story 3

Otto's First Birthday Celebration

1. Who is with Otto?
   ● his mom and the little otters
   ○ his dad and the ants

2. What did Otto's mom say?
   ○ Sit in the creek.
   ● Read this card.

3. Who did the otters need to see?
   ● Sid Seal
   ○ a camel

   The otters need to see ___Sid Seal.___

81

### PROCEDURES

For each step, demonstrate and guide practice as needed.

**Multiple Choice, Sentence Completion—Basic Instructions**
- Have students fill in the bubble for the correct answer.
- Have them write an answer in the blank and place a period at the end.

*Note:* You may wish to remind students that they can look in their storybooks if they are unsure about the correct answer.

## SOLO STORY READING INSTRUCTIONS

Students read from their own storybooks.

## COMPREHENSION BUILDING:
## DISCUSSION QUESTIONS AND TEACHER THINK ALOUDS

- Ask questions and discuss text on the first reading when indicated in the storybook in light gray text.
- Encourage students to answer questions with complete sentences.
- If students have difficulty with a comprehension question, think aloud with them or reread the portion of the story that answers the question. Then, ask the question again.

## PROCEDURES

### 1. First Reading

- Mix group and individual turns on student-read sentences. On individual turns, gently correct any error, and then have the student reread the text.
- After students complete the first reading and before the second reading, have students practice a paragraph. First demonstrate expressive reading for students, then give individual turns. Acknowledge student efforts.

### 2. Second Reading

- Mix group and individual turns, independent of your voice.
  Have students work toward an accuracy goal of 0–2 errors.
  Quietly keep track of errors made by all students in each group.
- After reading the story, practice any difficult words.
- If the group has not reached the accuracy goal, have the group reread the story, mixing group and individual turns.

### 3. Repeated Readings
#### a. Timed Readings

- Once the accuracy goal has been achieved, have individual students read the page while the other children track the text with their fingers and whisper read.
  Time individuals for 30 seconds and encourage each student to work for his or her personal best.
- Count the number of words read correctly in 30 seconds (words read minus errors). Multiply by two to determine words read correctly per minute. Record student scores.

#### b. Partner Reading

During students' daily independent work, have them do Partner Reading.

#### c. Homework 2

Have students read the story at home. (A reprint of this story is available on a blackline master in *Read Well* Homework.)

STORY 4, SOLO

## CHAPTER 2
# Meet the Seals

Remember, the otters are on a scavenger hunt. [1] What are they looking for? [2]

Otto was sleek and swam well.

He swam with a whoosh and a swoosh.

He could twist in the wet sea.

Soon Otto could see rocks in the sea. Otto said, "Look! See the seals on the rocks."

The little otters nodded. A little seal swam to meet them.

38

❶ **Summarizing**

❷ **Identifying—What, Who** (They are looking for clues that will lead them to a treat; they are looking for Sid Seal.)

Otto said, "I'm Otto Otter. We need to see Sid Seal."

The little seal said, "That's cool. Sid is my dad. He is on the rocks. Let's swim to the rocks."

Why do the otters want to see the little seal's dad?**1** What do they hope to find at the end of the scavenger hunt?**2** That's their goal—to find a treat.**3**

39

❶ **Inferring** (They hope he has a clue for them.)

❷ **Identifying—Goal** (They hope to find a treat.)

❸ **Teacher Think Aloud**

38

## RHYMING PATTERNS

Use work pages from the workbook.

UNIT 22 SKILL WORK ACTIVITY 4          Name _____ ✈
★ RHYMING PATTERNS: For use after Story 4

| (n)  ✗ (l) | (sl) (w) ✗ | (m) (wh) ✗ |
|---|---|---|
| **ot** | **eek** | **-y** |
| not | sleek | my |
| lot | week | why |

| (sm) (cr) ✗ | (m) ✗ (n) | ✗ (sh) (t) |
|---|---|---|
| **ash** | **eat** | **ell** |
| smash | meat | shell |
| crash | neat | tell |

82                                      © Sopris West Educational Services. All rights reserved.

**CHECKOUT OPPORTUNITY**

Listen to your students read individually while others work.

## PROCEDURES

Demonstrate and guide practice as needed.

### Rhyming Patterns—Basic Instructions

For each box, have students:

- Read the rhyming pattern.
- Circle the two sounds above the rhyming pattern that go with it to make real words.
- Cross out the sound that does not make a real word with the rhyming pattern.
- Write the two rhyming words on the lines provided.

*Note:* For students who struggle or who lack the English language base to know which are real words, you may wish to identify the two sounds they should circle in each box. Students can then write the pattern words on their own.

**❶ SOUND REVIEW**

**❷ NEW SOUND PRACTICE**

◆◆ **❸ FOCUS ON VOCABULARY**

**Review vocabulary word: "celebration"**

Have students review the word "celebration" and use it in a sentence. Say something like:
Remember, a celebration is often a . . . party.
When you graduated from [kindergarten], you had a graduation . . . (celebration).
When people have birthdays, sometimes they have a birthday . . . (celebration).

◆◆ **❹ SOUNDING OUT SMOOTHLY**

- For each word, have students say the underlined part, sound out the word, and then read the word. Use the words in sentences as needed.
- Provide repeated practice. Mix group and individual turns, independent of your voice.

**❺ ACCURACY AND FLUENCY BUILDING**

- For each column, have students say any underlined part, then read each word.
- Have students read the whole column.
- Repeat practice on each column, building accuracy first and then fluency.

*Note:* After students read the Airplane Column, ask them what is the same about "crack," "smack," "snack," and "whack." (They rhyme. They all end with /-ack/.)

**❻ TRICKY WORDS**

★ • Have students look at their new Tricky Word, "Listen." Remind them that a letter with a slash through it doesn't say anything.
- Have students sound out the word.
- Have students read the word three times and use it in a sentence.
- Have students read the row. Repeat, mixing group and individual turns, independent of your voice.

**❼ DAILY STORY READING**

Proceed to the Unit 22 Storybook. See Daily Lesson Planning for pacing suggestions.

**❽ COMPREHENSION AND SKILL WORK ACTIVITY 5 AND/OR ACTIVITY 6**

See pages 47 and/or 51.

◆◆ For ELLs and children with language delays, provide repeated and extended practice with the language patterns. See page 10 for tips.

UNIT **22** DECODING PRACTICE 3
(For use with Stories 5 and 6)

I. SOUND REVIEW  Use Sound Cards for Units 1–22 or Sound Review on Decoding Practice 4.

2. NEW SOUND PRACTICE  Have students read, trace, and say /ooo/.

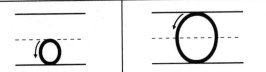

3. FOCUS ON VOCABULARY  Review "celebration."
See the Teacher's Guide for detailed instructions.

4. SOUNDING OUT SMOOTHLY  For each word, have students say the underlined part, sound out the word in one smooth breath, and then read the word.

■ not    rocks    on    mom

● Tess    last    hidden    seals

5. ACCURACY/FLUENCY BUILDING  For each column, have students say any underlined part, then read each word. Next, have students read the column.

| ✈ | ✏ | ✿ |
|---|---|---|
| crack | hoot | will |
| smack | shoot | well |
| snack | shoots | swell |
| whack | | shell |

6. TRICKY WORDS  Have students silently figure out each word and then read it aloud.

♥ ★ Listen    Where    Otto's    little

7. DAILY STORY READING

51

Sentence Suggestions: Use the appropriate suggested sentence *after* decoding each individual word.

### DUET STORY READING INSTRUCTIONS

Students read from their own storybooks.

The teacher reads the small text and students read the large text.

### PACING

- 2- to 4-Day Plans: Have students do the first reading of Duet Story 5.

  Then proceed to repeated readings of Solo Story 6.
- 6- to 10-Day Plans: Have students do the first *and* second readings as needed.

### COMPREHENSION BUILDING:
### DISCUSSION QUESTIONS AND TEACHER THINK ALOUDS

- Ask questions and discuss text on the first reading when indicated in the storybook in light gray text.
- Encourage students to answer questions with complete sentences.
- If students have difficulty with a comprehension question, think aloud with them or reread the portion of the story that answers the question. Then, ask the question again.

### PROCEDURES

**1. First Reading**

Mix group and individual turns on student-read sentences. On individual turns, gently correct any error, and then have the student reread the text.

**2. Second Reading**

Repeat the reading only as needed for comprehension.

STORY 5, DUET

## CHAPTER 3

### A Seal With a Big Nose

Remember, the otters are on a scavenger hunt.¹ What do they want to find?²

In no time at all the little seal and the otters were climbing onto the rocks in search of Sid.

# At last the little seal said, "This is my dad, Sid." At that, the little otters nodded. Sid was an elephant seal. Like other male elephant seals, Sid had a great big nose.

Do you think the otters have found their next clue?³ Is Sid a mammal that lives on the land and in the sea?⁴ Does he have a big nose?⁵

40

**VISUALIZING**

After discussing the gray questions at the top of the page, have students imagine the mammal the little seals are looking for. Say something like: Remember, the clue said the little otters were looking for a mammal that lives on the land and the sea.

Otto thinks it is a seal. Does a seal live on the land and in the sea? (Yes)

The clue also said the mammal had a very big nose. Close your eyes and imagine a seal with a very big nose.

Now look at the picture. Does that seal have a big nose?

❶ **Teacher Think Aloud—Summarizing**

❷ **Identifying—Goal** (A treat)

❸ **Inferring, Using Vocabulary—Clue**

❹ **Applying** (Yes)

❺ **Applying** (Yes)

Sid waddled over to meet the little otters. The otters and seals exchanged pleasantries for a bit.

Then Sid Seal said, "Otto's mom said I should read this card."

The little otters nodded. Sid said, "Listen. This clue will help you find your treat."

This is what the next clue said:

Dear Little Otter Detectives,

You did swell.
I hope this note finds you well.

Search the sea for this creature.
She has a really special feature.

She shoots ink when she's scared,
And changes color when she's dared.

She has eight legs as a rule.
This creature is really cool.

—Otto's Mom

What were the clues in the note?❶

Tess said, "That's strange. I can't think of a mammal with eight legs."

41

❶ **Identifying—What, Using Vocabulary—Clue** (The clues were to look for a sea creature that shoots ink, changes color, and has eight legs.)

Rod said, "It is not a mammal."

Then Tess said, "Not a mammal?

Tee hee.  I see.  Then this isn't hard.

She shoots ink. She has eight legs! It's got to be Grandmother Octopus!"

One little seal joined in the search.

At last Tess said, "There she is.  She is hidden in the rocks, and she has a card."

With that, Grandmother Octopus slid from the rocks. "Welcome," she said. "I've been waiting for you. I also have a clue to read to you."

42

# This is what the card said:

Dear Little Detectives:

You've done swell.
I'm glad you're well.

For your treat, I did bake,
One terrific crab cake.

    —Otto's Mom
P.S. All you need to do is find me.

What was the surprise?[1] Where do you think the otters and the seal will find the crab cake?[2]

Otto said with pride, "Mom's crab cake is the best!"
What was the treat?[3] What do you think the little otters will do next?[4]

43

❶ **Identifying—What** (A crab cake)

❷ **Inferring, Predicting** (The crab cake will be back at Otto's house with his mom.)

❸ **Identifying—What** (The treat was a crab cake.)

❹ **Predicting**

## STORY COMPREHENSION

Use work pages from the workbook.

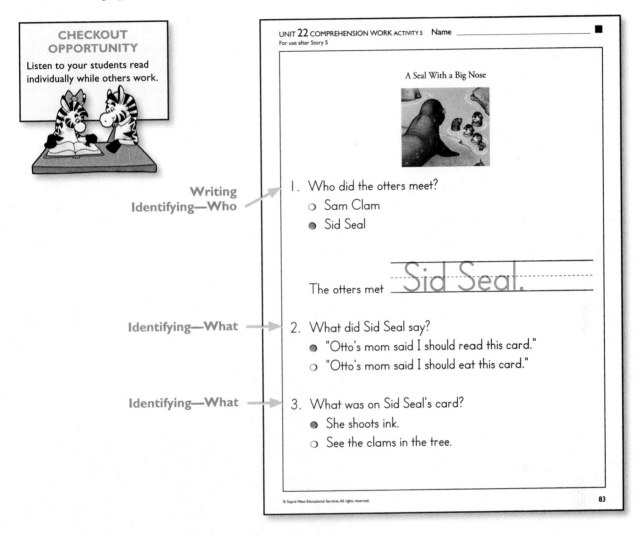

UNIT 22 COMPREHENSION WORK ACTIVITY 5   Name _____
For use after Story 5

A Seal With a Big Nose

**Writing
Identifying—Who**

1. Who did the otters meet?
   ○ Sam Clam
   ● Sid Seal

   The otters met _Sid Seal._

**Identifying—What**

2. What did Sid Seal say?
   ● "Otto's mom said I should read this card."
   ○ "Otto's mom said I should eat this card."

**Identifying—What**

3. What was on Sid Seal's card?
   ● She shoots ink.
   ○ See the clams in the tree.

83

## PROCEDURES

For each step, demonstrate and guide practice as needed.

### Multiple Choice, Sentence Completion—Basic Instructions

- Have students fill in the bubble for the correct answer.
- Have them write an answer in the blank and place a period at the end.

*Note:* You may wish to remind students that they can look in their storybooks if they are unsure about the correct answer.

## SOLO STORY READING INSTRUCTIONS

Students read from their own storybooks.

## COMPREHENSION BUILDING: DISCUSSION QUESTIONS AND TEACHER THINK ALOUDS

- Ask questions and discuss text on the first reading when indicated in the storybook in light gray text.
- Encourage students to answer questions with complete sentences.
- If students have difficulty with a comprehension question, think aloud with them or reread the portion of the story that answers the question. Then, ask the question again.

## PROCEDURES

### 1. First Reading

- Mix group and individual turns on student-read sentences. On individual turns, gently correct any error, and then have the student reread the text.
- After students complete the first reading and before the second reading, have students practice a paragraph. First demonstrate expressive reading for students, then give individual turns. Acknowledge student efforts.

STORY 6, SOLO

CHAPTER 4

## At Otto's

What did the seal and otters want to find?[1] Where did they go?[2]

Soon Otto's mom said, "Read my last card." The card said:

Who wants to eat this treat?

44

[1] **Summarizing, Identifying—Goal** (The seal and otters wanted to find the treat.)

[2] **Identifying—Where** (They went back to Otto's home.)

## 2. Second Reading

- Mix group and individual turns, independent of your voice. Have students work toward an accuracy goal of 0–2 errors. Quietly keep track of errors made by all students in each group.
- After reading the story, practice any difficult words.
- If the group has not reached the accuracy goal, have the group reread the story, mixing group and individual turns.

## 3. Repeated Readings

### a. Timed Readings

- Once the accuracy goal has been achieved, have individual students read the page while the other children track the text with their fingers and whisper read. Time individuals for 30 seconds and encourage each student to work for his or her personal best.
- Count the number of words read correctly in 30 seconds (words read minus errors). Multiply by two to determine words read correctly per minute. Record student scores.

### b. Partner Reading

During students' daily independent work, have them do Partner Reading.

### c. Homework 3

Have students read the story at home. (A reprint of this story is available on a blackline master in *Read Well* Homework.)

STORY 6, SOLO

"I do," said the seal.

"We do," said the otters.

"Me too," said Otto.

I think the little sea mammals deserve their treat.**1** What do you think?**2** Were they having fun?**3**

45

**❶ Teacher Think Aloud**

**❷ Inferring**

**❸ Inferring**

"Well then," said Otto's mom. "Let's eat this treat!"

Soon Otto's mom could hear, "Smack, smack, smack. What a sweet treat!"

The little seal said, "Otto, this was cool. Thanks!"

The little otters said, "Otto, this was neat. Thanks!"

Then Otto said, "Thanks to my mom. Thanks, Mom, thanks!"

Why did Otto thank his mom?**1** Did Otto have a good birthday?**2**

TEACHER THINK ALOUD
**Making Connections, Responding**
After completing the page, say something like: I liked this story because Otto appreciated all that his mom had done for him. Did you like this story? Why?

46

❶ **Inferring, Making Connections** (She made him a crab cake; she gave him a party.)
❷ **Inferring**

## SENTENCE COMPREHENSION

Use work pages from the workbook.

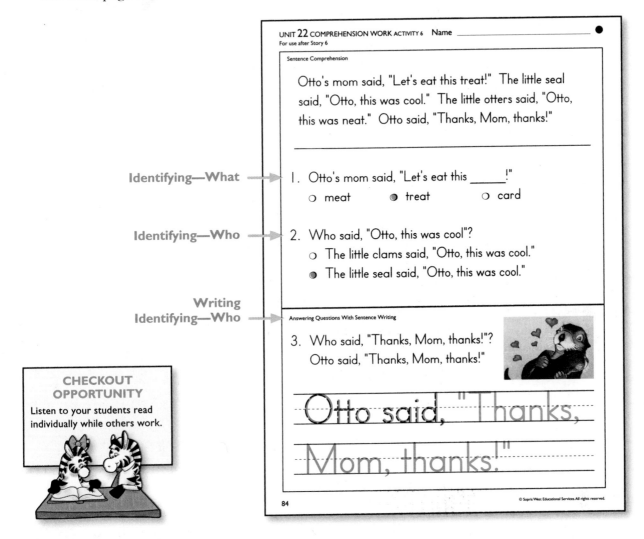

Identifying—What

Identifying—Who

Writing
Identifying—Who

UNIT 22 COMPREHENSION WORK ACTIVITY 6    Name _____
For use after Story 6

Sentence Comprehension

Otto's mom said, "Let's eat this treat!"  The little seal said, "Otto, this was cool."  The little otters said, "Otto, this was neat."  Otto said, "Thanks, Mom, thanks!"

1. Otto's mom said, "Let's eat this _____!"
   ○ meat        ● treat        ○ card

2. Who said, "Otto, this was cool"?
   ○ The little clams said, "Otto, this was cool."
   ● The little seal said, "Otto, this was cool."

Answering Questions With Sentence Writing

3. Who said, "Thanks, Mom, thanks!"?
   Otto said, "Thanks, Mom, thanks!"

Otto said, "Thanks, Mom, thanks!"

84                                                  © Sopris West Educational Services. All rights reserved.

**CHECKOUT OPPORTUNITY**

Listen to your students read individually while others work.

## PROCEDURES

For each step, demonstrate and guide practice as needed.

**1. Sentence Comprehension, Multiple Choice—Basic Instructions**

Have students read the sentences and answer the questions.

**2. Answering Questions With Sentence Writing— Basic Instructions**

- Have students read the question and answer.
- Have students trace the beginning of the sentence and complete the sentence.

*Note:* You may wish to remind students that a sentence begins with a capital and ends with a period.

*Note:* There are multiple uses for Decoding Practice 4.
- Use the Sound Review rows in place of Sound Card Practice.
- Use the whole page at the end of the unit for fluency building and/or to informally assess skills.
- Have students complete the page as a partner review.
- Build spelling dictation lessons from the sounds and words on this page.

**❶ SOUND REVIEW**

**❷ ACCURACY AND FLUENCY BUILDING**

**❸ TRICKY WORDS**

**❹ DAILY STORY READING**

See Daily Lesson Planning for story suggestions.

---

**WORDS CONVEY MEANING**

As students learn to decode words, your attention to meaning will help students make connections with the words they are reading.

• Throughout the decoding lessons, use the words students are reading in sentences.

• Have students use the words in sentences.

• Ask students what the words mean.

---

UNIT **22** DECODING PRACTICE 4
(See Daily Lesson Planning for story suggestions.)

1. SOUND REVIEW  Demonstrate an appropriate pace. Have students read the sounds in each row.

| ■ | O | c | h | ar | L | ea | r | | 7 |
| ✿ | -y | T | oo | w | i | d | a | | 14 |
| ♥ | Sh | ĕ | m | o | k | l | ee | | 21 |

2. ACCURACY/FLUENCY BUILDING  For each column, have students say any underlined part, then read each word. Next, have students read the column.

| ✈ | ✈✈ | ✿ | ✿✿ | ✿✿✿ |
| --- | --- | --- | --- | --- |
| h<u>o</u>t | w<u>ell</u> | cost | l<u>i</u>ttle | clean |
| tot | swell | lost | s<u>e</u>ttle | clock |
| lot | shell | loss | r<u>a</u>ttle | clam |
| cot | smell | moss | d<u>oo</u>dle | slam |
| dot | tell | moth | n<u>ee</u>dle | sleek |

> **RECOGNIZING RIMES**
> **(Reminder)**
> Recognition of the common visual patterns in the words helps facilitate speed of word recognition. The Airplane Columns help students chunk these rimes. With each reading of a column, increase the pace.
>
> Say something like:
> I think you can read the first airplane column about this fast . . . hot, tot, lot. Now it's your turn to read the whole column.

3. TRICKY WORDS  Have students silently figure out each word and then read it aloud.

| ☆☆ | listen | one | into | could | What | | 5 |
| ☆☆ | there | look | hasn't | two | was | | 10 |

4. DAILY STORY READING

52

# End of the Unit

## In this section, you will find:

### Making Decisions

As you near the end of the unit, you will need to make decisions. Should you administer the Oral Reading Fluency Assessment or should you teach Extra Practice lessons?

### Unit 22 Oral Reading Fluency Assessment

The Unit 22 Oral Reading Fluency Assessment is located on page 56 and can also be found in the *Assessment Manual*.

### Certificate of Achievement

Celebrate your children's accomplishments.

### Extra Practice

Lessons and blackline masters for added decoding practice and independent work are provided for students who need extended practice opportunities.

# Making Decisions

## ASSESSMENT READINESS

Assess when students are able to easily complete decoding tasks from the beginning of a lesson.

- If you aren't sure whether students are ready for the assessment, give the assessment. Do Extra Practice lessons if needed.
- If students are not ready for the assessment, proceed to Extra Practice lessons. Administer the assessment as soon as students are ready.

## GENERAL ASSESSMENT GUIDELINES

- Assess all students.
- Assess each child individually.
- Score student responses on the Student Assessment Record, adhering to the scoring criteria in the *Assessment Manual*. Use a stopwatch to time how long it takes the student to read the oral fluency passage.
- Follow the general instructions at the bottom of each assessment. Record a Strong Pass, a Weak Pass, or a No Pass.

## ACCELERATION

- If students read with 100% accuracy and exceed the fluency goal, consider shortening units.
- If an individual student reads with greater fluency than others in his or her group, consider regrouping.

## INTERVENTION OPTIONS—INDIVIDUALS

1. Add informal practice throughout the day.
2. Add practice with repeated readings on Solo Stories.
3. Find ways to provide a double dose of *Read Well* instruction.
   - Have the student work in his or her group *and* a lower group.
   - Have an instructional assistant, older student, or parent volunteer preview or review lessons.
   - Have an instructional assistant provide instruction with Extra Practice lessons.
4. Consider placement in a lower group. If one child's fluency scores are significantly lower than the other children in the group, success will be impossible without additional and intensive practice.

## INTERVENTION OPTIONS—GROUP

1. Extend the unit with Extra Practice lessons.
2. Consider a Jell-Well Review before moving forward. (See the *Assessment Manual*.)

## CERTIFICATE OF ACHIEVEMENT

When students pass the assessment, celebrate with the Certificate of Achievement. Then, set a personal goal. (See *Getting Started*.)

**TRICKY WORD WARM-UP**

| two | his | should | wanted | there |
|-----|-----|--------|--------|-------|

**ORAL READING FLUENCY PASSAGE**

## A Nest

★ What do we see?  We see a nest.　　8

Where is that nest?  It's in the tree.　　16

Where is that tree?  It is on a rock.　　25

Where is that rock?  It's not on land.　　33

It is in the sea.　　38

| ORAL READING FLUENCY | Start timing at the ★ Mark errors. Make a single slash in the text (/) at 60 seconds. Have student complete passage. If the student completes the passage in less than 60 seconds, have the student go back to the ★ and continue reading. Make a double slash (//) in the text at 60 seconds. |
|---|---|
| WCPM | Determine words correct per minute by subtracting errors from words read in 60 seconds. |
| STRONG PASS | The student scores no more than 2 errors on the first pass through the passage and reads a minimum of 52 or more words correct per minute. Proceed to Unit 23. |
| WEAK PASS | The student scores no more than 2 errors on the first pass through the passage and reads 41 to 51 words correct per minute. Proceed to Unit 23 with added fluency practice, or provide Extra Practice lessons in Unit 22, and/or provide a Jell-Well Review. |
| NO PASS | The student scores 3 or more errors on the first pass through the passage and/or reads 40 or fewer words correct per minute. Provide Extra Practice lessons and retest, and/or provide a Jell-Well Review. |

# Certificate of Achievement

## This certifies that

_____ ,

on this _____ day of _____ , ____ ,

has successfully completed

## *Read Well* Unit 22

**Sounds Mastered:** s, e, ee, m, a, d, th, n, t, w, i, Th, h, c, r, ea, sh, k, -ck, oo, ar, wh, ĕ, -y (as in "fly"), l, o

**Known Words: By Unit 21, you had learned and practiced 347 words.**

**New Words Mastered in Unit 22:** camel, listen, mammal, mammals, otter, otters, Otto, Otto's, clam, clams, clean, clock, cost, cot, doodle, dot, hidden, hot, lend, loss, lost, lot, mom, moss, moth, needle, nodded, not, on, rattle, rock, rocks, Rod, seal, seals, settle, shell, shoots, slam, sleek, smooth, Tess, tot, twist

**You can now read 391 words—plus many other words made up of the sounds and patterns you've learned.**

Note: Personal and Team Goal Setting forms can be copied from Units 16 and 17, or from *Getting Started*.

**1 SOUNDS**

Have students say each sound.

**2 WORD DICTATION**

Have students count the sounds in each word with their fingers, identify and write each sound, and then read the word. Use the words in sentences as needed.

***we, tree, and, land***

The first word is "we." Tell me the word.  (we)
We're going to count the sounds in "we."
Tell me the first sound. **Hold up one finger.**  (/www/)
Tell me the next sound. **Hold up two fingers.**  (/eee/)
How many sounds are in "we"?  (Two)

Tell me the first sound.  (/www/) Write it.
Tell me the next sound.  (/eee/) Write it.
Do Smooth Blending.  (/wwweee/) Read the word.  (we)

Repeat with "tree," "and," and "land."

**3 SENTENCE COMPLETION**
**That is not a *rock*.**
- Have students read the beginning of the sentence with you.
- Dictate the last word "rock."
- Have students trace the dotted words and complete the sentence with a period.
- Have students read the sentence.

**4 ACCURACY AND FLUENCY BUILDING**
- For each column, have students say any underlined part, then read each word.
- Have students read the whole column.
- Repeat practice on each column, building accuracy first and then fluency.

**5 TRICKY WORDS**
Repeat practice, mixing group and individual turns, independent of your voice.

**6 DAILY STORY READING**
Proceed to Extra Practice Activity 1.
- Have students read each sentence from the book.
- Repeat, mixing group and individual turns, independent of your voice.

**7 EXTRA PRACTICE ACTIVITY 1—CHECKOUT OPPORTUNITY**
Have students fold, color, and read the book.

> **CAUTION**
> Your children may not need Extra Practice. If in doubt, assess students and include Extra Practice only if needed.

> **DICTATION**
> - Demonstrate and guide practice as needed.
> - Have students check and correct.

> **BUILDING MASTERY**
> **(Reminder)**
> Throughout Extra Practice, demonstrate and guide practice, but only as needed.

**I. SOUNDS** Have students say each sound.

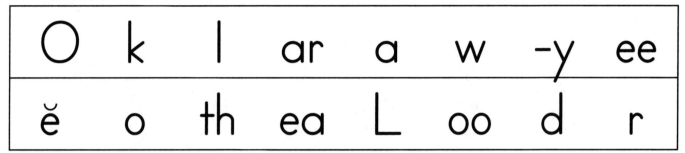

| O | k | l | ar | a | w | -y | ee |
|---|---|---|----|---|---|----|----|
| ĕ | o | th | ea | L | oo | d | r |

**2. WORD DICTATION** Have students count the sounds in each word, identify and write each sound, and then read the word: "we," "tree," "and," and "land."

I _____    2 _____    3 _____    4 _____

**3. SENTENCE COMPLETION** Have students read the beginning of the sentence. Dictate "rock." Have students trace the words and complete the sentence with a period.

That is not a

**4. ACCURACY/FLUENCY BUILDING** In each column, have students say any underlined part, then read each word. Next, have students read the column.

| ♥ | ♥♥ | ♥♥♥ |
|---|----|-----|
| <u>on</u> | land | <u>weeded</u> |
| m<u>o</u>m | lĕnd | <u>needed</u> |
| n<u>o</u>t | lĕt | nodded |
| r<u>o</u>ck | nĕt | <u>rested</u> |
| r<u>o</u>cks | nĕst | <u>twisted</u> |

**5. TRICKY WORDS** For each word, have students silently figure out the word, then read it aloud.

| do | look | one | A | Where |
|----|------|-----|---|-------|

**6. DAILY STORY READING**

Otters and Seals

Seals are sea mammals 4

too. Seals swim in the sea 10

and rest on the land. See 16

the seals on the rocks. 21

Seals are sleek and 25

swim well. The seals can 30

swim with a whoosh and a 36

swoosh! 37

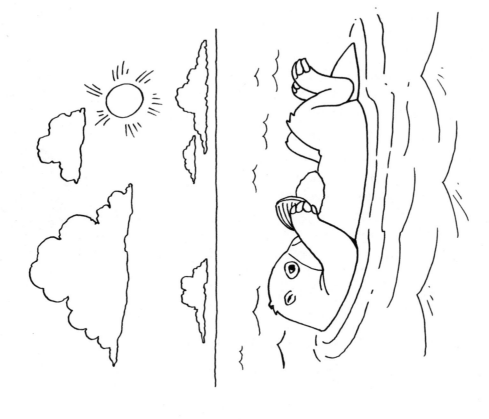

Otters are sea    3

mammals. Otters swim,    6

eat, and rest in the sea.    12

Otters are sleek,    15

smooth, and clean. See    19

them twist in the wet sea.    25

Otters eat clams in the    30

sea. See the otter hit the    36

clam with a rock!    40

**1 SOUNDS**

Have students say each sound.

**2 WORD DICTATION**

Have students count the sounds in each word with their fingers, identify and write each sound, and then read the word. Use the words in sentences as needed.

***nest, not, rock, that***

The first word is "nest." Tell me the word. (nest)
We're going to count the sounds in "nest."
Tell me the first sound. **Hold up one finger.** (/nnn/)
Repeat with /ĕĕĕ/, /sss/, and /t/.
How many sounds are in "nest"? (Four)

Tell me the first sound. (/nnn/) Write it.
Repeat with /ĕĕĕ/, /sss/, and /t/.
Do Smooth Blending. (/nnnĕĕĕssst/) Read the word. (nest)

Repeat with "not," "rock," and "that."

*Note:* Tell students to spell the /k/ in "rock" with <u>ck</u>.

**HAVE STUDENTS CHECK AND CORRECT.**

**3 SENTENCE COMPLETION**

***Mom* sat in the tree.**

- Dictate and have students write the first word, "Mom." Remind students to begin the first word of the sentence with a capital letter.
- Have students read and then trace the dotted words to complete the sentence.
- Have students read the sentence.

**4 ACCURACY AND FLUENCY BUILDING**

- For each column, have students say any underlined part, then read each word.
- Have students read the whole column.
- Repeat practice on each column, building accuracy first and then fluency.

**5 TRICKY WORDS**

Repeat practice, mixing group and individual turns, independent of your voice.

**6 DAILY STORY READING**

Proceed to Extra Practice 2 Fluency Passage.
- Have students read each sentence.
- Repeat, mixing group and individual turns, independent of your voice.

**7 EXTRA PRACTICE 2 FLUENCY PASSAGE—CHECKOUT OPPORTUNITY**

As you listen to individuals read the story, have students color the picture.

Name_____

1. **SOUNDS** Have students say each sound.

| m | c | oo | ĕ | K | wh | l | o |
|---|---|----|---|---|----|---|---|
| h | L | ea | n | ar | i | O | t |

2. **WORD DICTATION** Have students count the sounds in each word, identify and write each sound, and then read the word: "nest," "not," "rock," and "that."

1 _____    2 _____    3 _____    4 _____

3. **SENTENCE COMPLETION** Dictate and have students write "Mom." Have students read and then trace the words to complete the sentence.

_____    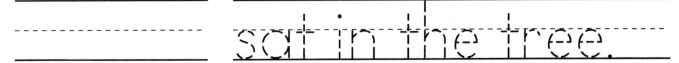 sat in the tree.

4. **ACCURACY/FLUENCY BUILDING** In each column, have students say any underlined part, then read each word. Next, have students read the column.

| ♥ | ♥♥ | ♥♥♥ |
|---|----|-----|
| n<u>o</u>t | clean | on |
| h<u>o</u>t | clock | Don |
| sh<u>o</u>t | clam | Dan |
| d<u>o</u>t | slam | děn |
| l<u>o</u>t | sleek | měn |

5. **TRICKY WORDS** For each word, have students silently figure out the word, then read it aloud.

| should | is | What | there | wanted |
|--------|-----|------|-------|--------|

6. **DAILY STORY READING**

Name_____

## FLUENCY PASSAGE

### Mom's Room

I went into Mom's room.  I needed a          8

rest.  I could not rest.  There was a little     17

red clock in Mom's room.  I had to              25

listen to that clock.  Tick tock.  Tick tock.   33

My goal is to read with 0–2 errors. This is what I did

Have students read the sentences. Time individual students for 30 seconds; mark errors. To determine words correct per minute (wcpm), count words read in 30 seconds, subtract errors, multiply times two, and record on the chart. If student completes the passage in less than 30 seconds, have him or her return to the top and continue reading. (Repeated readings may be completed with older students, assistants, or parents.)

| Reading | 1st | 2nd | 3rd | 4th |
|---|---|---|---|---|
| Errors | | | | |
| Words/ 30 seconds | | | | |
| wcpm | | | | |

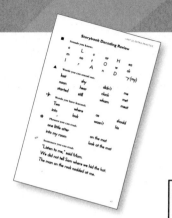

### ❶ STORYBOOK DECODING REVIEW

For each row, mix group and individual
turns, independent of your voice.

### ❷ SOLO STORY REVIEW—UNITS 19 AND 20

- Guide student reading, gradually
  increasing rate.
- Mix group and individual turns on the
  stories, independent of your voice.
- Repeat practice. While one student reads,
  have others track the text with their fingers
  and whisper read.

---

**CAUTION**

Your children may not need
Extra Practice 3 and 4. If in
doubt, assess students and
include Extra Practice only if
needed.

---

### ❸ EXTRA PRACTICE ACTIVITY 3—CHECKOUT OPPORTUNITY

- Have students cut out the Letter Cards and arrange them on the top row
  of the Letter Card Grid to create the words "on," "not," "hot," "tot," "lot,"
  "lock," "rock," "let," and "net."
- Have students arrange and glue the letters in the remaining rows to
  create "not, "hot," and "rock."

*Challenge Activity:* With the remaining letters, have students make a
word in the blank row.

### ❶ DECODING PRACTICE 4 REVIEW

For each row, mix group and individual turns, independent of your voice.

### ❷ SOLO STORY REVIEW—UNITS 21 AND 22

- Guide student reading, gradually increasing rate and
  emphasizing expression.
- Mix group and individual turns on the stories, independent of
  your voice.
- Repeat practice. While one student reads, have others track the
  text with their fingers and whisper read.

### ❸ EXTRA PRACTICE ACTIVITY 4—CHECKOUT OPPORTUNITY

- Have students cut out the Memory Cards. While students are cutting
  out their cards, listen to individuals read a Solo Story.
- Once the cards have been cut out, have the group or pairs of students
  play Memory.
  Using one set of cards, spread the cards out in rows with the words
  facing down.
  Have students take turns. Each time a card is turned over, have the
  group or pair identify the word.
  If the words match, have students set the pair off to the side.
  If the words do not match, have students turn the cards back over and
  try again.

| | | |
|---|---|---|
| o | o | o |
| t | t | t |
| e | n | r |
| h | l | ck |

Name_____

Letter Card Grid

| | | |
|---|---|---|
| | | |

| | o | t |
|---|---|---|
| h | | t |
| r | | ck |

| | | |
|---|---|---|
| was | tree | land |
| was | tree | land |
| rock | on | the |
| rock | on | the |
| Mom | in | in |

*Note:* Memory Cards can also be used to create sentences. Also, please note that there is no match for the word "Mom."